WARRIOR OF THE MIND AND WITHIN

WARRIOR OF THE MIND AND WITHIN

AUTHOR CHARLOTTE RAMEKA
Caitlin whiteshaw, Charlotte rameka

978-0-473-62094-3 987-0-4473-62096-7

CONTENTS

WARRIORS OF THE MIND AND WITHIN BORDERLINE PERSONALITY DISORDER (BPD)

Someone once asked me to be curious, so now I ask you to be curious and form your opinion. If you could look beyond a diagnosis, would you? If you could look past someone's flaws and past mistakes, would you? If you could look past society's views and stigmas to form your own understanding, would you?

In this book I am asking you to be curious and open minded. I want to crush the stigma that is held around Borderline Personality Disorder. This diagnosis is very mis-represented. I want to educate people in what it's like to live with this challenging disorder. I also want to give the word 'borderline' less power over individual perception.

Borderline Personality Disorder

Borderline Personality Disorder, [BPD] is a brains response to trauma that a person has endured, this can be for a lot of reasons. It creates a person to become very dysregulated this means they struggle to process their emotions and they can feel and respond to daily life in extreme measures. They can often switch through their emotions very quickly and feel things much more intensely then other people. Because of the trauma people go through, the brain begins to create a narrow tunnel.

It creates things to look very black or white. It also creates trust and abandonment issues. People with trauma experiences often find it hard to maintain relationships. They find it extremely hard to manage and control their thoughts of experiences from their past. They often relive their trauma in environments/situations, where they feel at risk of feeling the same emotions. Coping with trauma is extremely hard to do . People with BPD often resort to extreme measures to escape their pain, but this is detrimental and often leaves them feeling worse than before they acted on their emotions. I know this is a lot to process, but I don't want to give a false idea that is not true. There is a wide range of ways people can deal with their urges and impulses as everyone's situation is different. People can resort to self-harming, alcohol and drugs, not eating or restricting what they eat, some people can develop tics, some people overwork themselves to the point they cannot work anymore, anxiety and depression can often have a huge impact and occasionally some can attempt suicide as they feel they have no way out. Sadly, the reality is some people do lose their lives.

Caitlin whiteshaw

hope

"There is hope, even when your brain tells you there isn't." ——
John Green
This diagnosis can be treated and you can recover.
The hurdles of BPD can be overcome. There are other people fighting this battle everyday alongside you. I hope the following content give you some sort of hope that you can break free from the mental chains that are placed and lodged in your brain. That you can live a full functional life. Know you can live without the pain you are currently experiencing, that your life is more than a diagnosis. Hope is planted by seeds that you and people who support you place down. They grow when you feed it. The same goes for positive actions and positive coping mechanisms. It takes a lot of work to recover but you can also look at it like recovery is a part of your life journey. You are resilient and with the right treatment and team and support, impossible things seem possible. It will feel impossible and unbearable but

fight through it. Get up and fight. And when you can't hold the hope others you trust can. They can help you fight for a better life.

Stigma

BPD has been very stigmatized because people lack the knowledge to understand this complex diagnosis. People form their opinions based on observed behaviours and not what are driving those behaviours or the trauma hidden behind the actions.As a society we are often very quick to put a label on something, but actually forget the fact we are all human we are equal that this diagnosis does not make us any less deserving. False conclusions are made that we attention seek but in reality, every minute is a battle and every second and urge surges past.Stigma can destroy progress and this way of thinking is very negative.I don't believe stigmas, I just open my eyes to what I am missing and the symptoms currently being presented. You can't possibly know ones pain but you can walk alongside them and help the see beyond the pain.

Charlotte rameka

Individual

No two people are the same when being diagnosed with an illness. People can present in very different ways. People need to understand that what makes up a journey for one individual can be similar but very different for another.

Diagnosis can hold a heavy label in our society because categorising is in our nature if you tick the box and the symptoms and get diagnosed you are now expected to act in a certain way. This is absolute bullshit!!!!! Yes, diagnosis can give us answers, but it should not rule ones opinion and definitely should not define you or your future or you as a person.

It should also never be a way that people can ignore a person or say they cannot do something. People can become successful for so many other ways, not just if they have money. You as an individual have a purpose no matter what your circumstances.

Relationship with yourself

When we become an adult a lot of us struggle with the fact that in our lives we are the main character, but in others we are not. When you add BPD to the mix things become a lot more complicated. Someone reminded me that the relationship with yourself is far more important than having lots of friends.

Learning to accept yourself is a challenge, because as humans, we are our worst critics. This trauma-based illness makes us as people question everything we say and do to the point of destruction. Telling ourselves we are not worthy- but this is because we have trouble sitting with our own company. For a lot of people, they have been mistreated so they only see themselves in a negative light.

For me I struggle to sit with myself, but I am now learning to tolerate being with myself, to do things on my own, like make decisions for myself and care for myself. It's not easy at all and it takes a lot of patients and self-kindness.

I started by making my bed each day, so I had a tidy bed to go to sleep in.

Then I started doing things I use to take interest in , like singing, walking, dancing and art. I could see my struggle because I was critical about everything I did and if it wasn't good enough I would immediately stop or rip it up. But I tried again and again, I would use some breathing techniques to help calm my thoughts. I would also use grounding techniques like focus on 5 things I can see then 4 things I could hear 3 things I could touch 2 things I could smell. This allowed myself to calm the anxiety's I had when I was by myself.

It's important that we learn to tolerate our own company. Another way I have found its easier to sit with myself is learning to diffuse from my thoughts. Acknowledging they are there and valid, but accepting I am not my thoughts and they don't define me. Now I understand this might appear straight forward but it's not. To change the way, we view ourselves is really not an easy task- in fact it will really challenge you. Changing a thought or view point takes practise and repetition. It's something you are going to have to work on. Starting with small self-care tasks and working your way up is the best way to challenge the thoughts. Another way you can change the way you see yourself is looking and relating to positive affirmations. These can be useful in getting yourself to think more positively.

A Day in life with someone with BPD

I am 23 female, as well as being diagnosed with BPD, I also struggle with Complex Post-traumatic Stress Disorder [CPTSD], Depression and Chronic Suicidality. I try to focus on symptoms not diagnosis, so I don't stigmatize myself.I need you to be curious when I write the following. A main symptom is feeling excruciating pain for being alive and overwhelming thoughts, which makes me feel completely numb and empty like I'm locked away feeling nothing. This will seem odd and you may come to an opinion its fake, but I can tell you it's not please don't invalidate something you haven't walked through.

Impulsiveness and risk-taking behaviours can increase within seconds and quite often sneaks up and then builds up overtime. For me I often miss my early warning signs, not because I don't care but because I have another thinking brain and it plays tricks on me. I worry about everyone's safety before myself. I am incredibly hypervigilant and sensitive when it comes to other people.

I like to help and support others because I never want someone to feel the pain I feel. People with borderline have a huge compacity for empathy towards others. But this means they lack the ability to take care of themselves and their energy for self-care is impaired. Distorted thoughts and feeling of the world and one self are a massive thing I struggle with. I often find it hard to grasp reality. It's like I see the world in a different light. When I have an experience that's similar or associated to my trauma it results in me reliving the whole trauma and often results in an increase of risk-taking behaviours. For people with complex mental health backgrounds, if these experiences are left and not talked through, it can build until eventually a person will explode as feel like they either not seen or weren't heard. People with BPD excessively apologise for things they have never done because they feel uneasy in a relationship and continuously think they are doing something wrong. I really struggle to see my existence is a positive thing so I apologise to people for doing things- I convince myself I have done to them. I often feel people are going to leave me so if I withdraw first I tell myself it's in their best interest as the fear of abandonment is so real, I can't put in words how terrified I get of people leaving my life. Trust is something I battle with constantly because as a child I never had someone I could learn to develop trust with. In saying that its completely the same with relationships I never learnt it, so I'm constantly treading water in relationships worrying if I'll fail someone.

Validation is super important for everyone. Validation is something that makes us feel heard and listened to. Some times when we feel unheard we automatically assume no one cares about us. Sometimes people project their feelings on us and then we repeat the same, this transference is super unhealthy and can become very overwhelming for both parties. Being touch like patted on the shoulder hugged or form off contact can be extremely triggering for someone that has been abused. People do not often tell people its triggering, because they don't want to upset the person, but also we want that affection. For me I have certain people I feel comfortable with hugging and some not. I know I am picky but it's based on a build-up of trust.

Validation

People that struggle with BPD often feel alone and not listened too. People see the behaviours and forget that it's the thoughts the pain and agony that forces someone to act on an urge. But if someone took an extra five minutes to listen to someone and validate their emotions things would be a lot easier. A person can feel heard and respected it doesn't make everything go away but it makes it that much easier to cope with -knowing you aren't alone.

People with BPD need to learn to validate others too. Validation is something the community should be trying encourage. For example, If we all taught younger children the rewards of validation, when they are older they can accept, understand and provide validation to others.
Validation can impact our brain to signal whether a person is listening and when someone is actively taking part of a conversation.
Validating yourself is not an easy task, because we constantly judge ourselves but it can have such a positive impact if we do.
To help me validate myself I do a lot of gratitude journaling to recognise the things I am grateful for or that I appreciated in my life.

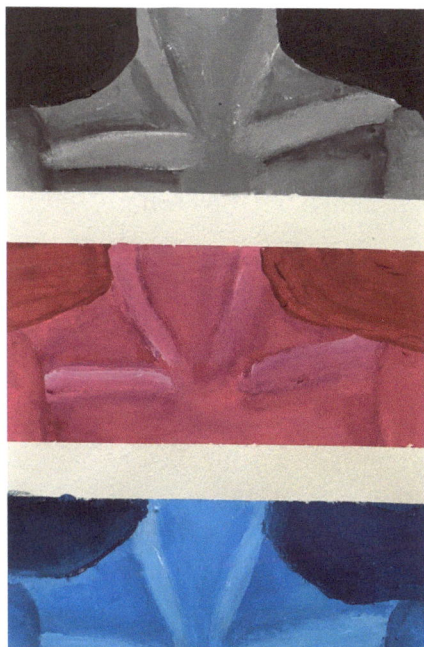

Charlotte Rameka

This allows myself to see the positive things that I have and allows me to see that the positive experiences can cancel out the negative and uncomfortable ones that I may have.

My advice- I know It's very scary to feel okay sometimes, but by allowing yourself to feel validated can put you in such a better mindset.

Relationships

I have never really learnt how to maintain a relationship with people.

My life has been extremely inconsistent making friends and keeping them has been a very big struggle. At the age of 23 I am just learning how to have stable and meaningful relationship and I can defiantly say it's not easy. I still constantly ask for reassurance or over apologise, because I don't want to mess up the only good friendship I have. People that struggle to trust will put their faith into one person and when the trust is broken there's no going back. The trust is gone often people who suffer with BPD can't see past trust broken.

To help someone who's struggling with these relationships, please don't treat them any different. Learning to sit with uncomfortable feelings are very hard at first but sometimes we need to learn to sit with them.

People with BPD feel emotions very intensely and when people break promises or give up this makes them feel extremely worthless and hopeless -this can lead to them being triggered.

we generally wear our heart on our sleeve because a lot for us is all or nothing which is black and white thinking pattern which is a hard concept to grasp sometimes.

Setting boundaries with people is a very normal skill but for people with borderline personality disorder really struggle to balance boundaries in relationships. A way you can help someone through setting boundaries is to sit with them and be transparent, to be open minded and to be patient. They may not see your point of view straight away but give them the space to process the things you have discussed with them and talk it through so they understand. This may take time. Sometimes reassuring someone and allowing them to ask question is the best way to open up better communication.

Dialectical Behavioural Therapy [DBT]

DBT is a well-known tool that is taught and used in treatment for BPD but is also used for people who struggle with intense emotions. It teaches the skills and awareness of one's self.
The four foundations of DBT are mindfulness, interpersonal effectiveness, distress tolerance and emotion regulation.
I wish I could say this is a walk in the park but honestly, it's not. This challenges a person in ways I can't describe. It pushes you to stare your fears head on. It also makes you evaluate and self-critic your behaviours and thoughts at the same time.
These are skill to help people regulate and have more control and self soothe. Riding the emotional wave is exhausting but the skills and awareness to your thoughts is something we could all learn. It is not easy and challenges the brain to challenge and change our response to distress.

Society

People struggle to grasp the concept that the behaviours mask the excruciating pain and emotional dysregulation someone is dealing with. Society tells us the way we should think and feel and act, but actually we are as a collective in charge on how we view things we need to stop pressuring people to confine to something they are not. Communities need to learn to support and be aware, this is the only way we will stop things like suicide. For our growing population suicide is becoming a way of escaping pain and trauma . We can do more for our community and help people through crisis but it starts in the home and school.

It starts when we are kids learning about emotions. It is totally okay to have emotions and to feel, but it's what we do with it and how we manage the emotions that is so important. Being heard, understood and validated needs to be seen as an essential requirement in child development.

Our communities are where we can make this awareness, teaching everyone how to respond to distress and using coping mechanisms such as music, nature, beach and sensory tools.

Things I feel need to be addressed is the labels people place on people with BPD. Things like attention seeking, manipulative, difficult and selfish -these are very far from the truth in fact this person is fighting their own war in the head and these words can really impact a person's ability to recover.

People need to be careful that they have not misinterpreted the situation because they haven't looked past the behaviour that a person has presented with.

People need to ask themselves why is this person reacting and resorting to these unhelpful coping behaviours. Validate their pain. If they want to change the way they react to their emotions there is plenty of help available. They can always ask their GP for assistance with this. If they do not have a general practitioner they can use a 24/7 line 1737 text or call. Always go to the local emergency department if you or another person have immediate medical concerns and also take a note of your local crisis line to reduce the crisis from escalating to self-harm behaviour.

Professionals

Well where do I start. To be completely honest it is a catch twenty-two not everyone we interact with is positive and helpful. I have learnt really fast that I could only really depend on myself to keep going. Emergency mental health services were a life saver for me because they not only went above and beyond for my welfare but challenged my darkest thoughts I knew when I contact them that they would be transparent and that I was respected.
They had been there for me when I couldn't see a future or when I was dissociated and unregulated I owe them so much.
But here's the catch people quite often find it extremely hard to trust and talk to someone they never meet which is understandable. I find there could be better ways of communicating rather than they asking blunt cold questions. I find inpatient unit for mental health is a complicated situation. Because trust is such a hard thing to give and from both ends its hard to get along with everyone but learning to tell someone you don't know your struggling is pretty difficult. I to this day still find it hard and I have had a lot of admissions and now know staff well, Yet I still always resort to my negative coping mechanisms. This is not only frustrating for me but the staff too. And it doesn't help them understand my thought processes.
Sometimes I am judged by this and I am often left feeling alone and misunderstood. I get frustrated that no one can see my pain but I mask it so I am currently learning to approach staff instead of resorting to self-harm. I know this isn't only something I struggle with. The thing is the staff can't read our minds and not every nurse is going to understand, but you must persist with the recovery path as they will soon see

the work you are putting in. The reality is, we don't all get along as humans, personalities clash and some staff have different intentions, but we need to take charge of our recovery and step above the negativity.

This can be challenging and bring up a lot for people that have been through past trauma. A good thing to keep in mind is that at the end of the day the staff are there to do a job. Working with them and not against them is going to only help you but it's going to help form healthy working relationships.

A big thing I stand for is reminding myself that professionals are also human we can't expect them to solve our every problem, it's not possible but explaining your thought processes and why you feel these feelings are your best chance at getting someone to understand what you are trying to work through. Sometimes you are going to hear the reality of your situation and although you may not agree with them they are only trying to make your aware of your presentation so that you can see the effect your behaviour is impacting not only yourself but the people around you. I can say you won't always see eye to eye but try to listen and open the mind to what they are trying to tell you. But I do encourage you to speak up if you feel you are not being heard or feel misunderstood. The best way to do this is to be calm and explain what is going on for you. I can say myself that is something I have always struggled with is articulating how I feel. Sometimes it's hard to put it into words but they are they are only there to help. Yelling and raising your voice only escalates the situation and I can say from experience that you only end up in more emotional pain and more agitated. This will not help them understand your pain.
Paranoid feelings

People the struggle with BPD find it hard when others are feeling strong emotions as they often think it's something they have done to the person but in reality it has nothing to do with them. This can occur by just a glance or someone staring into space -it is hard to not feel at fault. These type of events that occur in society for me leave me feeling responsible. Silly right? But I feel the intense emotions to the point of injuring myself as I blame myself. It replays over and over and I am very bad at letting things go. And then it's become a trigger for my suicidal thoughts. Other people can feel like something they have done is wrong and can obsess over it. If I can give advice for this, it is not to tell someone they are silly or invalidate them. The best thing is to listen and try and get them to see that it can't possibly be true ask them questions be curious into why they feel that intensely. If the person can find it within themselves to see beyond the thought then they are likely able to move and work through this.

Another thing people experience when they feel like things are their fault is constant guilt this can be overwhelming and bring them down. They become less confident around people. This can create isolation. People can also feel like someone is constantly in their space watching their every movement. They may experience the feeling of paranoia, This can also create isolation or feeling alone.

Self-harm

Self-harm is more than damaging your body it goes deeper then the skin -this is such a broad topic!
Now I am not going to encourage this as for someone who has struggled with this and now chronically acts I want you to understand why someone turns to self-harm and how you can reach out to someone who may be at risk. I am not stating ways as it might become an idea for someone I do not promote that at all.
So self-harm is a coping mechanism it's not a healthy one, but it fills the void or releases the feelings someone is experiencing. Its driven

purely by being overwhelmed and in pain or anxious or not happy within themselves. Sometimes it's to feel something.
There are honestly so many things that drive self-harm listen to the person. Don't instruct them to listen -then suggests strategies they could try instead. Maybe offer to try with them.

Carrying out a positive coping mechanism is more beneficial if they feel they aren't alone. Sometimes trying something new with the person who is trying to stop self-harm is the best way to help them through- although at the end of the day it's there responsibility to change.
They have to want to give it up. It is definitely not easy it is very challenging and will bring up obstacles for them. For example there may be a moment where they struggle more with regulating their thoughts when they stop harming.
Another thing to keep in mind is that people can become very hateful towards themselves because of the actions they have resorted too, this is normal. Not judging a person is crucial when trying to encourage them who ca then refer onto a councillor or more help if required

Suicidal ideation

Imagine not being able to escape your own mind constantly ! how would you feel?
Suicidal ideation is very common in people who battle BPD, they often feel there's no hope, no way out, alone ,in a lot of emotional pain and believe that things will not get better. They lose a sense of identity. These feelings are often felt very strongly and drive them to attempt or succeed in suicide.

I have been told a lot I am at risk of accidental risk of death. At first I was very offended by the term accidental death. But hear me out. Our waves of emotions can go from 1 to 10000 in a second if we can learn to ride it out then we can change the statement.

I found I was offended because the thing is, I have moments of wanting to die because I don't see it getting better and I have no idea of who I am.

My past trauma makes me feel like an alien and I feel I don't belong. But I can empower myself to get through this. I don't have to live in this much pain.

It is a real battle and struggle. Its tiring, Its exhausting and it will challenge every fibre of you, but then hopefully you'll have some sort of life back in control. This is done in many different ways. Suicidal ideation is horrible but if you stick at recovery you can do this.

I know It can feel as if everything is stacked against you. If you have immediate concerns for \someone's safety you need to get them help as sometimes a person is in so much pain the cant see a way through the darkness. It can be dangerous. Making a permanent decision for what can be a temporary problem means they would miss out on so much if their life ended and let's not forget the impact on those around them.

"I understand your pain. Trust me, I do. I've seen people go from the darkest moments in their lives to living a happy, fulfilling life. You can do it too. I believe in you. You are not a burden. You will NEVER BE a burden." — *Sophie Turner*

Impact

living with a mental illness in reality doesn't only a\ffect the person struggling it impacts there whole life circle. Family, family friends, teachers, workmates, support networks.

Sometimes people don't realise the impact they have on those around them. That their actions could turn someone's world upside down.

Now I'll let you in on a secret, I thought I was unlovable and a burden, that people would be better off with me gone.

There would be no more E.D visits no more money wasted in my recovery -that I didn't see working. Memories of being escorted by police and appointments after appointments.

But the reality was I could not see that it was the opposite in fact the world had more for me to experience then pills, then psych ward admissions and countless hospital visits.

So, there is a massive catch. I am only learning I am not perfect in fact I'm understanding the impact of my mistakes on those around me.

I can always show them I am going to try to change and learn and grow that's the best gift I can give those around me. But something we need to learn about ourselves is people often see the good in us when we can't and we need to realise that our actions do impact other people be it in a good or bad way.

Something I like to keep in mind is if I was the other person how would I feel. Sometimes this can help but generally it's up to individual person not others.

The key, Learn to not project your emotion s onto other is extremely important and is something I definitely wish I could have learnt earlier. Sometimes we do this unintentionally but at the end of the day it happens. We need to own it because people can only handle so much. They have their own struggles to- don't ever forget that.

They have daily stresses, family stresses and insecurities. Other people are human too.

Not letting go

Holding on to things that have happened to us is a big trauma response because it takes us back to places we don't want to remember and this can trigger PTSD, CPTSD attacks and flashbacks. It takes you right back to young ages where you were let down and then that creates the same feeling in the now.

Learning to be present and in present time is defiantly hard but something we need to learn to manage the self-harm and suicidality. DBT skills can definitely be useful here as it's a tool amongst many tools to cope with distress. Sometimes people can experience black or white thinking which creates another barrier. Black and white thinking can be developed through trauma because if you fell constantly the way you do and have been told things repeatedly you develop a way of thinking that doesn't allow you to see beyond the trauma or beliefs you have developed. This is not letting go of historic sayings because you can't see beyond what people previously told you or showed you. Unfortunately for people it's an ongoing battle that is definitely not a quick fix.

Learning to trust in the reality is something that takes practise you have to constantly remind yourself of where you are, who you want to be and where you want to go in life and holey shit it's a mission let me tell you.

But sometimes telling someone your insecurities can help. Ask them what they think. Talk to someone you trust talk to someone you know is going to tell you the truth

Emotional waves

So, pain isn't just physical it's also emotional and when riding out emotions it can feel like the whole world is going to collapse at your feet. It feels never ending and like things couldn't get any worse or it's never going to leave. This is FALSE it can get better and boy sometimes

I feel this very pain too. It consumes all your energy and takes over the mind be let me remind you it will pass it won't feel like it and you will feel like you have to act but the truth is if you do the trauma the pain wins. You deserve a lot better than that.

To conquer this is so individual and the way people get through this its determination, support. And skills. I will have a skills page in the book to help you learn some skills to try. Make sure if you are feeling like this at least one other person knows so they can support you. And you have to be ready to change and want it again we are only human we may make mistakes and get it wrong but it's how we come back and what we learn from our mistakes. You might also find the person your supporting makes a mistake or takes a step back -don't get angry step back and say what can we do now and what can within ourselves do to stop this. The harsh reality is that we cannot control what others do and how they respond we can only dictate our own actions and response this is done with a great deal of patience and practise. But we can also reach out to someone to sit with us to help us ride the wave although it's impossible to have someone 24/7 so learning to do this ourselves will be super important. The reality for people living with BPD is that when we are dysregulated we cannot see a way through- which makes it extremely hard to see that it will pass. We need to learn for ourselves that it will pass if we learn the strategies that are offered. We also need to make the conscious effort to change our pattern of how we deal with situations. This is really hard and it's a battle of the mind but is very much achievable. The best treatment for this is DBT it will help not only the person struggling with bpd but also the people that are supporting them.

Skills

A skill I can say have definitely influenced me is the triple A's. The triple A's stand for Awareness Acceptance and Action.

Awareness is the start of change if you can't acknowledge there is something not right you can't begin the process to stop the behaviour or thought pattern. This is extremely important to see the things within ourselves and say it.

Acceptance if you cannot accept what is starring you in the wrong direction you can't fix it. Acceptance also comes that maybe what someone resort to is unhealthy this is a massive achievement in itself. There will be many self-judgments when it comes to this but you just need to remind yourself you are in the process of change and that it may take time.

Action so you may need to plan with someone that knows you well or with any of your support systems or if you feel confident on your own so that it has the best chance of it becoming a positive outcome.

Then step by step go through the motions here you will find your mind will challenge you replacing a habit is a difficult thing to do and it's definitely not easy but it is so possible. You are limitless. You are brave. You can do the things you put your mind to. I believe in you.

There are many skills that you can learn to help you battle the mind. DBT will set you up with an very good range of skills. Connecting with a Psychologist can help. They can also teach skills in a wider range which they see will be beneficial for you.

Having a case manager or keyworker helps as they can actively go through skills with you. You can research yourself on google and they have a wide variety of skills.

Here's the thing I am not going to lie not every skill will help or work but you will find some that will and you need to be consistent and try things for a period of time to allow the brain to make the new pathways. Everyone is very different so the same skills won't work for everyone because we are all so wired differently we need and require different needs. I can say confidently that there are skills that will work. Also wanting to change and being ready to change is a massive.

Making goals

A big part of recovery is making small goals that you can achieve that will help enhance your wellness. When we get unwell sometimes little things like drinking enough water, showering, brushing teeth and eating becomes over whelming. But doing these thing are essential to our wellbeing. They are the staple things that help us function. We as human beings need goals to keep us working towards something this is something very individualised and you will find your goals won't be in line with others THIS IS OK. It's okay to be on your own wave length. Naturally we compare ourselves to what is expected of us or what others have but realistically this isn't healthy we need to make goals for ourselves for our progress not others.

This is hard to do so start small. Build yourself up then expand from there. From another perspective if you are supporting someone who is making goals you need to be mindful to be focused on their input not what you want. Sometimes we do this without being aware as we naturally want what is best for someone but being mindful this isn't your goals its someone else's. learning to engage in healthy habits will allow the person to feel more positive about their future. It creates moments of hope. Hope can really have a big impact on someone's recovery.

Change

Change is not easy to change a behaviour or a way of thinking. It can be overwhelming and bring its challenges. Our brains are very complex and starting a new pathway in our brains is definitely not easy. Sometimes people resort back to what they know because although its unhealthy it works. But in the long term it is just not sustainable. When helping someone change it will bring up a lot for people I think the best thing a person can do is be there show up and continue to support and remind them that they can successfully change their habit.

The length of which it takes to change a behaviour is dependent on the person, their willingness to change and their support. It may be up and down because we all make mistakes we all go backwards before we go forward.

Please, if your supporting someone through change remind them it's okay to feel your emotions and they are valid. Reminding them that this hard work will pay off and things won't feel so challenging forever will help them keep going. To whoever is trying to change something keep at it. At the end of the day the work you put in will determine the gains you will make I know this sounds blunt but to be upfront no one can change it for you, you have to make the change. I am speaking from experience in the past I expected change to fall on my lap this isn't the right mindset.

I had to learn that hard work, persistence, determination and being consistent.

I learnt that it feels extremely uncomfortable and uneasy and can really play on my mood but I chose to keep at it as I didn't want to do that behaviour anymore I wanted to face my fears front on. I wouldn't have been able to do it without the support. I am still learning every day. But it is possible.

Acceptance

Acceptance is a scary word that can be interpreted in so many ways. In this context to accept oneself is a massive and ongoing journey. When we are unwell sometimes we act in ways that is not normal for us or in way we wish to deal with things. We are left with the aftermath of our actions. This can bring up guilt and also make us feel ashamed and more isolated. The way forward is what steps you decide to take next.

First before we can change we need to learn to accept that what we did was unhelpful to our wellbeing. We can learn to accept but not forget and that is totally okay in fact it's in human nature. Accepting yourself is important but a challenging thing and it can be something that we constantly are working on no one is perfect no one has all the answers. We are all working on things some people are faced with more challenges but the way I like to look at it is it makes us not only stronger but allows you to view the world differently.

By making mistakes we learn lessons that allow our mind to asses situations from an open perspective. We as humans are constantly learning how to approach the world and I can say from expectance its far from easy but it's an essential part of life. If I can give any advice is take the opportunity to reflect and be curious.

Asking for help

Don't ever be ashamed for being you. Asking for help does not mean your weak, it certainly doesn't mean your uncapable and it doesn't define who you are. Everyone needs help at some point in their life and its okay. It's okay to not have the answers for everything in fact people don't reach out enough because the stigma is unrealistic. Also beginning to open up is hard and you will feel uncomfortable but try to procced with it and stick at it. I know for some people they see it as a sign of weakness but in fact it's a sign of strength. Asking for help is essentially telling people what support you need to be able to continue to function.

Learning to do this will come of great benefit to your recovery as communication is so crucial to recovery and is something I wish I opened my mind up to earlier. We as humans function better when we reach out and articulate the things we need. Sometimes we expect people to know we are struggling or that something is wrong because naturally we want someone to rescue or save us but this isn't in your or anyone's best interest. I know this is hard concept to grasp but saying what you need is far more important because than whoever is supporting you knows exactly what your needs are.

Set backs

Setbacks are perfectly normal! It's how we grow and learn although it feels uncomfortable and you may judge yourself everybody has set backs or relapses. We as humans are far from perfect we make mistakes and take steps back but that does not mean you have done something wrong or you're a bad person take it from a different perspective take it as an opportunity to do something different
To explore a different side to thing explore what is still troubling you. Don't expect that you should do everything on your own.
A setback is something that if you share what's going on it will help you feel less isolated. also support helps make things shared. They say a problem shared is a problem halved. This is so very true. Sometimes when we relapse we can't see things clearly talking to someone you trust will help you bounce back from this.

Moving forward

In moving forward there are some things that might occur that you're not expecting. Unfortunately, you will see that some of your friendships and relationships with others may be detrimental to you recovering which you may have not been able to see while you were unwell. Sometimes we have to make some difficult choices and let go of some people that are holding us back. This I must say is still the hardest thing I find in my recovery because letting people go is hard even the ones you love.

But you cannot continue to live the way you use to if you want things to change and its hard. We as people sometimes fantasies acceptance that isn't going to come from other people but only ourselves. I strongly feel if you are wanting to do this you need to be ready to cope with how you're going to feel going through this process. It's going to challenge your thoughts about yourself and who you are. Bear in mind where you are trying to get to and that at the end of the day you are creating a healthier you.

Sometimes moving forward means leaving things behind. I am really starting to see the benefits of this in my life I don't constantly feel under pressure I don't constantly feel like I am walking on egg shells and I no longer feel like I am suffocating myself to fit in a space I shouldn't. it's hard but it is defiantly worth it. I am now learning to find my worth and I hope that for you. I hope that after you have really worked on yourself that you see the benefits you deserve.

Caitlin whiteshaw

Things no one mentions

People that struggle with BPD struggle with always feeling guilty. They struggle to separate their thoughts from reality and constantly feel \guilty for the way they are. But generally, they won't voice this because they don't want to put pressure on other people so they sit with this uncomfortable feeling. This can often drive the person to act impulsively as the cannot tolerating sitting with this feeling. Quite a lot of people that suffer from borderline personality disorder feel like when they are trying to communicate their feelings they often feel like they are not understood and speaking another language. But this is a catch twenty-two because often we withhold all of our feelings because we are scared to commit to fully opening up.

This can sometimes occur when as children people are not listened to or heard which ingrains in us that we cannot trust people. Imagen having third degree burns over about 90% of your body lacking the ability to protect yourself and if we think of this in the context of mental illness lacking the emotional skin that at the slightest touch or breeze, movement or touch the absolute pain you would feel this is how intense people with borderline personality disorder feel. This is very real.

See the thing is about this illness is people hide their pain to not burden those around them but then that can have suffer some very significant consequences.

As humans we cannot deal with everything on our own. But some-time when people feel mentally down they lack the ability to see a point in confiding in someone because everything seems so foggy.

Last message

Recovery is a choice and not an easy one at all. It will challenge every fibre of your being but you are worth it. Please remind yourself it's okay not to be okay that it's okay to cry and that its okay to ask for help but just don't stay in that funk pull yourself out get back up and try again.

There's a life just waiting for you if you choose it and it will be a beautiful one. Realistically we all have up and downs it is in human nature. I believe that the challenges will become more bearable and your start to see the life you want. You can create it and live it don't lose hope there is always lessons to be learnt and that's okay.

If you are reading this I am proud of you. I am proud that you decided to be curious proud that you took the time to read and under-stand some pretty heavy stuff. If you are a family member be patient and don't give up on your loved one. If you're a friend support them but remember we are all human.

Please don't ever give up hope and curiosity because you deserve to be on this earth just like anyone else. Life throughs curve balls but I know for myself I have met some truly amazing people that who have taught me so much. Who have fought for me when I did not see a future. They gave me my life back and that's the best gift someone can give you. I am still learning but I know by sharing this it could help someone the way others have helped me. Please don't give up you have a purpose.

Acknowledgements

Thank you to

Psychiatrist Melanie Strydom
She was my inspiration for this book she has believed in me when no one else has and has really given me another shot at life and in-dependence. she also always explained in depth why I was going through the feelings I was experiencing this is a massive help to help me develop insight. She encouraged me to purse this book and the amazing idea about writing something I am so passionate about. We share the same feeling that this subject is not really talked about and that awareness would help so many people. I cant thank her enough for the opportunity.

Thank you to

Tessa Harbutt, Shannon golder, Cushla Cameron, Zena, Di Cowan they helped and supported me doing this book. But also has had a big part in my recovery. Their teeime and effort was life saving for me. They gave me the time when they were listening and were very patient but also always instored hope that things could get better for me if I chose it they have given me are real chance in moving forward and doing what I am passionate about.

Thank you to

Caitlin whiteshaw
She has produced to amazing art pieces that have been shown in this book. But she has given me the strength to purse this book. Caitlin has been my rock. Learning to trust was very hard for me but Caitlin has been nothing but patient and there for me.

Thank you

Charlotte Ross
My gp she has been there for me through it all always trying to keep me safe and has never given up on me.

Thank you

To my professional team
To Nancy, pam, Georgia, gabby, donna, Shannon, Adrienne
They have encouraged me throughout this process and are helping me on my journey I am very greatful for that.

Thank you

Te whare mahanga and ashburn for being vital parts of my journey. I am hoping to return to ashburn to finish my trauma therapy and get the help I need. These two have taught me a lot and open my mind. I am hoping to return to finish my therapy.

Thank you

to acc for there ongoing support while I am unable to work and allowing me to have time to get treatment.

About writer

Hi my name is Charlotte aroha rameka. I am the oldest of 8. I have struggled with my mental health most my life being diagnosed with clinical depression, complex post traumatic stress disorder (cptsd), borderline personality disorder and chronic suicidality. I am still very much on the road to recovery and far from perfect but I have seen so many things and always kept my eyes wide open. I have encouraged myself to always be open minded and learn about the things I find challenging because I don't want to continue to be in the same cycle or place I was in. I defiantly am one of those people who always have learnt the hard way because I am very stubborn and sometimes struggle with reality but I have grown a lot stronger in what I want for myself, who I want in my life and the fact I am still alive. I feel extremely lucky being 23 because I still have so much to offer the world and I don't want someone to be in that dark hole I was. It is not reality but if I can help someone by publishing this book I would feel so humble that they took the time to read it.my next steps is to return to a treatment centre Ashburn and focus on getting well and healing I. am excited foree that. My message is invest in yourself and give yourself a chance to live before doing anything that will be permanent because you deserve to be here. You are not a burden. You deserve to be in the world. You can make a difference too. I have written this as a tool for anyone who needs this book. don't struggle alone reach out to people they may not understand at first but they will if u give them time. I am so proud to everyone who is fight the battle of there minds because its extremely painful.

Art produced by Caitlin whiteshaw & Charlotte Rameka
Photgraphy by Charlotte Rameka

Thank you for reading